I0416477

Elder Cool Time

A Time to Teach

A Time to Weep

A Time to Laugh

A Time to Embrace

The Purpose-Evolving Life Filled with
the Fears, Tears, and Cheers in Facing
and Embracing the Aging Process.

JOHN H. GREEN, PH.D.

© Copyright 2006 John H. Green.
All rights reserved. No part of this publication may be reproduced, stored in a retrieval system, or transmitted, in any form or by any means, electronic, mechanical, photocopying, recording, or otherwise, without the written prior permission of the author.

Note for Librarians: A cataloguing record for this book is available from Library and Archives Canada at www.collectionscanada.ca/amicus/index-e.html
ISBN 1-4120-9076-8

PUBLISHING™
Offices in Canada, USA, Ireland and UK

Book sales for North America and international:
Trafford Publishing, 6E–2333 Government St.,
Victoria, BC V8T 4P4 CANADA
phone 250 383 6864 (toll-free 1 888 232 4444)
fax 250 383 6804; email to orders@trafford.com
Book sales in Europe:
Trafford Publishing (UK) Limited, 9 Park End Street, 2nd Floor
Oxford, UK OX1 1HH UNITED KINGDOM
phone 44 (0)1865 722 113 (local rate 0845 230 9601)
facsimile 44 (0)1865 722 868; info.uk@trafford.com
Order online at:
trafford.com/06-0832

10 9 8 7 6 5 4 3 2

Comments

Dear John,
Thanks so much for letting me preview *Elder Cool*. You're on to something! It's so important to embrace this aging-thing (many don't get the privilege) and to do it by giving folks food for thought.

> Cathy Brown, Executive Director of Council on Aging, St. Johns County, St. Augustine, Florida

John,
I added one Proverb to my part. Use it if you wish. The article by you is good.

Proverb 4:23 – "Keep thy heart with all diligence, for out of the heart come the issues of life." Keep your heart with clean thoughts... remember it begins with a thought, then words, then action, then habits, then character, which determine your eternity.

> Bobby Bowden, Head Coach at Florida State University, Tallahassee, Florida

John Green's teaching has always focused more on how to live or how to make good decisions than learning facts for an exam. Wisdom is more than the gaining of experience; it is learning from those experiences and helping others apply the lessons of life to their choices and beliefs. We are all teachers. Whether we focus on teaching as we interact with our children, parents, and friends, or through others observing our behavior; we are teachers. *Elder Cool Time* will allow John to extend his teaching far beyond his classroom, where students honored him as Professor of the Year. May we learn from his wisdom and his "Religiosophy" and teach others as we lead our lives through the Elder Times.

Dr. Glen Moore, Provost, St. Johns River
Community College, St. Augustine, Florida

In Memory

This book is dedicated to the memory of my Mother and Father, Ollie Gafford Green and John Lawrence Green.

Acknowledgements

I would like to express appreciation to several friends for assistance in writing this book. First, I would like to thank my friend, and former colleague in ministry, The Reverend Larry Cook. He has been a friend for over twenty-five years. I consulted with Larry relating to scripture and format. Larry is the best joke teller. However, sometimes I can't put them into print! Thanks also to Susan Ross, a colleague, and teacher of Humanities at St. Johns River Community College. She was very helpful in assisting me with organizing, brainstorming, and structuring the material, often over a cup of highly caffeinated coffee. Also a colleague, Bill Kiernan, helped with some final computer skills that my *Computer For Dummies* book did not include. I would like to express gratitude to my friend, Linda Easom, Assistant Principal at John Carroll High School in Fort Pierce, Florida, for editing my work with the detail and diligence of my former major professor!

My hat is off to Charlie and Nancy Hamilton. They are friends who provided me with the inspiration to continue through difficult times and embody the true meaning of elder cool. Charlie has a saying, "if you're friend or kin, no matter the sin, I'll help you if I can." A few years ago The Reverend Doctor Hamilton suffered serious strokes, and yet, he and his wife Nancy have managed to live through the struggles, and remain mentors and teachers to others.

I must give thanks to my wife, Kay, who has lived up to the marriage vows, "for better or worse, for richer or poorer." Kay's artistic talents helped the book's cover.

Kay's fulltime profession is with the Council on Aging.

Although I am a step-father, for over twenty-four years, Kay and the children have always been respectful and caring. Daughter Robin, MA degree, is married to Chris Bowman, PhD, and they have two children, Kate and Elie. Son Bryan, Engineering Degree, and his wife Nicole, Engineering Degree, have a daughter named Sienna. The three grandchildren call us Mamaw and Papaw. As you might imagine, we are delighted to open to them our hearts and our checkbooks!

Contents

Preface

A Time for Every Matter

"For everything there is a season, and a TIME FOR EVERY MATTER under heaven: a time to be born, and a time to die; a time to plant, and a time to pluck up what is planted; a time to kill and a time to heal; a time to break down and a time to build up; a time to weep and a time to laugh; a time to mourn, and a time to dance; a time to cast away stones, and a time to gather stones together; a time to embrace and a time to refrain from embracing; a time to seek and a time to lose; a time to keep, and a time to throw away; a time to tear, and a time to sew; a time to keep silence, and a time to speak; a time to love, and a time to hate; a time for war, and a time for peace."

Ecclesiastes 3:1-8 (NRSV)

"The all-wise, All-knowing God cannot speak without meaning many things at once."

Cardinal Newman

Religiosophy

I have coined a word, *RELIGIOSOPHY*. The coin has two sides: religion and philosophy. The definition I give to the word is simple. RELIGIOSOPHY is the conforming of practical wisdom to religious thoughts with a sense of humor. The material the coin is made of is humor. If you have not closed this book by now, let me explain some more.

Wisdom Literature

Wisdom Literature from the Old Testament is generally recognized in the books of Job, Proverbs, Ecclesiastes, and some of the Psalms. Some Wisdom Literature has existed since the Ancient Greeks and the Egyptian Empire, even before the written knowledge of the Old Testament. Let it be known also that some of the Wisdom Literature in the Old Testament and from the ancients has some strange similarities.

The Old Testament Wisdom Literature provides insight into how to live a productive life along with the realities of fears, tears, and cheers. Ecclesiastes, in particular for me, teaches the wisdom of a purpose-evolving life and the wisdom of a purpose-evolving faith. In other words, there is truth that the teacher teaches and, in turn, the teacher learns about life and faith during this evolutionary process.

Life, for the author, is often an act of futility involving the pain and suffering that one encounters due to the inequalities of justice in life.

Yet, he views life as a learning time, not only a time to weep but a time to laugh. The author is too pessimistic for some but realistic for others in the sense that life includes pain, suffering, and inequalities with some opportunities for humor.

OVER THE HILL

Ecclesiastes is the transliteration of the Greek name which in Hebrew is called *Kohelet*. (Believe me, I did not coin this word!) In plain English, one who speaks to an assembly of religious folks, perhaps one who is a Preacher or who is a Teacher. Most scholars agree the author was past middle-age. Definitely he was over the hill. Now middle-age then could be different from the present. Since so many people live to be a hundred years old today, middle-age could be fifty! That makes me feel younger. Past middle-age designation simply adds to the credibility for speaking words of wisdom as taught by the author of Ecclesiastes.

Purpose Of Life

What is the purpose of Life? That's an age-old question to which I would like to suggest our purpose is to teach. The author does not imply that everyone should be a teacher as he is, and that our purpose in life is to teach. However, my suggestion is allow the author to become an example for us, and let each of us become a teacher. Each one teaches differently and may not have an assembly or classroom as the author, *BUT BY WORD OR BY DEED WE ARE TEACHING SOMEONE SOMEWHERE.*

Teacher

"Besides being wise, the Teacher
also taught the people knowledge,
weighing and studying and arranging
many proverbs."

Ecclesiastes 12:9 (NRSV)

My RELIGIOSOPHY is that since the Teacher

teaches, why can't the students follow? My
RELIGIOSOPHY is that the purpose of life evolves
into teaching. Teaching gives us a purpose and meaning to living. Each teaching day will bring a challenge, comfort, and material different from the day
before. And, if you add a bit of humor to the life process, success in learning how to live and how to give
becomes an enriching feeling of happiness regardless
of your state in life. Teaching is living and giving.

MYSTERY BOOK

Ecclesiastes has been referred to by some scholars
as a dangerous book, a difficult book, and a mys-
tery book. Others, I do know, call the book a mistake
for being in the Old Testament at all. Some of my
Christian colleagues have real problems "fitting" the
book into their faith. That's the real mistake!

TIMELESS

Why not let the words simply speak for themselves to
people in whatever stage or faith they are in life? No
matter the age of a person or the time frame of his-
tory, time is always a factor in living through the bad
times and the good times. The words, for example, of

Ecclesiastes on the subject of time, shall we say, are timeless? It is the subject of time that I have chosen to use as a stepping off place for the context of this book project.

SENSE OF HUMOR

"Many heretics would have been saved if they had had a sense of humour."

Michael O'Carrol

This book project is not intended to communicate in any way a detailed exegesis of scripture, but to use chosen scripture as a source of wisdom and faith for the present and the future. One learns from the past and, thereby, learns to prepare for the future. In the context of time the purpose of this project is to embrace the aging process with a sense of humor based on the importance of wisdom and faith. A sense of humor without the reality of pain, hurt, and disappointment is unrealistic.

Humor, in itself, is not the total answer. On the other hand, a sense of faith, along with a sense of humor, is a pivotal point that can provide a sturdy foundation and a steady direction through the quagmires of life.

AGONY AND ECSTACY

The purpose-evolving life accepts that one needs a purpose, but the purpose may not come to light until one accepts becoming a teacher. You will become a teacher REGARDLESS OF WHETHER YOU CHOOSE TO OR NOT. And whether the teaching is good or bad depends on the teacher. A teacher of what, you may ask? That's the joy and excitement evolving in the journey of life. Everyone has a journey, whether a long or short one. Ecclesiastes teaches us the agony and the ecstasy of life's evolving journey and the journey determines what one believes and what one teaches.

Ecclesiastes teaches the disappointment and frustration of wasting one's time on wealth, pleasure, or sometimes, a religious matter. He concludes these may be an illusion of happiness in life. The answer to a meaningful life comes to one who willingly shares the disappointments and frustrations of life. When one learns the pains of the unsuccessful paths taken, then the paths out of the unsuccessful could become paths to the successful. The truly successful will realize their path is to TEACH wisdom learned from the paths ill-chosen and the paths well chosen.

Introducing Elder Cool

"That men may know wisdom and instruction, understand words of insight, receive instruction in wise dealing, righteousness, justice, and equity; that prudence may be given to the simple, knowledge and discretion to the youth—the wise man of understanding acquire skill, understand a proverb and a figure, the words of the wise and their riddles. The fear of the Lord is the beginning of knowledge; fools despise wisdom and instruction. Hear, my son, your father's instruction, and reject not your mother's teaching; for they are the fair garland for your head and pendants for your neck."

Proverbs 1:2-9 (RSV)

LET me introduce you to Elder Cool. You are Elder Cool if you decide in your purpose-evolving life to offer instructions to others. You have great knowledge based on the wisdom of aging. Elder represents a life-experienced teacher, and Cool is accepting the aging process with grace and dignity. You accomplish being Elder Cool by your actions as much as, or more so, by your words. You may not always be aware you are teaching others, and you may not always be in the mood to embrace your maladies, but if you set your attitude in motion that being Elder Cool benefits society, as well as your own better being, you may find yourself to be Elder Cool.

You are Elder Cool when you are more open and honest about the on-going aging process. At the same time you are determined to live a life of quality in spite of physical, social, financial, or emotional limitations. Elder Cool is grace under challenge. Elder Cool is when you embrace your maladies with courage. Elder Cool is not being embarrassed to ask for help in a time of need. Elder Cool is hanging the car keys up because you do not want to hurt yourself or others.

Elder Cool is refocusing the activities in your love life. Elder Cool is talking about the unmentionables such as funerals, finances, flatulence, and some, well, just unmentionables. Elder Cool is to be health smart, dress smart, and smell smart. You can be a leader in instructing others that elder bashing is not cool. This can be done with gracefulness. And the appreciation you receive from friends and family will make you Elder Cool. In the process you will teach them the wisdom of the ages.

I am sixty-five years of age at this writing. I have been diagnosed with IBM – Inclusion Body Myositis. This is a disease that attacks the biceps and leg muscles. The good news is that it is a gradual deterioration of the muscles. The bad news is that it cannot be reversed. I now have major trouble with maintaining my balance and, with the regular aging process, find myself with serious physical challenges. I include this condition in order to add credibility to my understanding of the aging process. I also try to add humor to serious situations.

This book project, some might say, is seriously humorous. The intent is not to make fun of the elderly, but to add that a sense of humor helps to cope with a very tough problem of adjusting to growing old. I am a fulltime teacher at St. Johns River Community College in St. Augustine, Florida, and feel that I am continuing to make a difference in life. You can make a difference in life by being a teacher and never enter a college or a classroom. Maybe it's time to be Elder Cool.

JUST A THOUGHT

"One may age without wisdom if one does not listen to the wisdom of the ages."

JHG

Pop Was Elder Cool

MY dad was eighty-seven years of age when he decided to visit several assisted living homes. One day Pop decided he was ready. At the ripe old age of eighty-eight, he phoned to say he had driven himself to the Advent Christian Village in Dowling Park, Florida, and checked into the assisted living facility. He parked his truck for the last time. I knew how much he enjoyed driving his truck, and his decision to park it had to be a tough one. Hanging up the keys to his truck for the last time was sad.

I found out later, when I was cleaning and preparing to sell his truck, that Pop had been ticketed for backing into a car in the Walmart parking lot. He was going to have to appeal or turn in his driver's license. He decided to hang up the keys. Elderly people find giving up the automobile one of the most difficult decisions of all because it is the last bastion of independence. However, to protect yourself and others, you might be Elder Cool to know when to turn in your driver's license. You will be a teacher to others.

ELDER COOL

YOU MIGHT BE ELDER COOL IF YOU KNOW WHEN IT'S TIME TO …

TURN IN YOUR DRIVER'S LICENSE

It might be time to turn in your driver's license if …

∞ On your last trip to Miami you drove on the interstate median more often than you did on the highway.

∞ You missed the Handicap Parking spot by three spaces.

∞ You have more dents in your car than Bayer has aspirins.

∞ Your friends will no longer ride in the car with you.

∞ You put your car on cruise control and go to sleep.

∞ There is no drive-thru at the convenience store, but you made one.

∞ You have become uninsurable because you have had more wrecks than a racecar driver.

∞ You have begun to express road rage in your own driveway.

∞ The Yield traffic sign became a challenge, and you lost.

∞ Your car was rear-ended by a van, and you didn't know it.

∞ Your last wreck involved hitting a Highway State Patrol Officer's car.

∞ The last three times you tried to stop, you pushed the gas pedal instead of the brake. The proof is that the hole in the wall of your garage is growing larger.

∞ You are receiving a finger gesture from other drivers on a daily basis.

∞ You have hit the same oak tree in your yard three times in a row, and you swear the tree moved.

∞ You drive so slowly it that takes you thirty minutes to negotiate over a speed bump.

∞ Your right hand blinker has been on for the last thirty miles.

∞ You parked your car in the garage only to realize you were at somebody else's house.

∞ You do not believe that the objects in the side view mirror are really closer than they appear.

∞ You ran over your neighbor's last three pets.

∞ You backed into a car in a Walmart parking lot at least once.

Land of Extreme Home Makeover

DON'T you just love it when deserving families get a new home either through the popular TV show on ABC or a Habitat home? It is even good when former President Jimmy Carter asks you for money in the name of Habitat for Humanity.

I am less excited when I see elderly people give up their homes because they can no longer afford them or have the energy to keep up the property. Or in some cases, the property taxes are increasing to the point that they are literally forced out of a home. Losing the right to drive is one hardship, but it does not compare to losing the home. However, there is another side of the coin when it comes to extreme home makeover.

Springing up around the states are senior citizen communities that I will refer to these as Geezervilles. Geezerville is my word for the senior citizen communities taken from the word "geezer." Surely you have heard a poorly placed sarcastic comment, "Look at that old geezer!"

The Oxford English Dictionary reveals the use of the word "geez" in a Shakespeare scene where the jester describes King Lear as "one who doth geez most nunkily." (As a speech teacher I have a great interest in words and their meanings.) I remember as a youngster hearing for the first time, "Damn that old geezer; he can't drive worth a crap."

In Florida, Geezervilles have become a way of life. For many growing old, this is an extreme home make-over. Billboards up and down the state of Florida depict the good life in Geezerville. I have noticed the billboards picture really beautiful older people sitting by the pool or in a spa. Sometimes they are pictured playing golf or shuffle board while smiling ever so happily. Emphasis is always billed on "active community." That means, I suppose, contrary to being an inactive community. After all, who would want to be in an inactive community, like say, a cemetery?

Let me tell you about my visit with my wife to

Geezerville and the initial desire for an extreme home makeover. I did not see any beautiful older people as pictured on the billboards. That was my first clue about truth in advertising relating to Geezervilles. I did see many smiling prune-skinned folks limping around the community park.

I can understand how young people think geezers will bore you to death. I was bored following and listening to the saleslady spill her memorized speech. She toured my wife and me in a golf cart and at the first stop we were shown this "lovely modular home." Back home we call that a trailer. She parked on a hill and forgot to put on the brake, so after exiting the cart, I turned to witness the cart making a fast getaway. I guess the cart had had enough of "modular homes."

Next we were taken to the swimming pool. Looking around for some "hotties" like I had seen on the billboards, I saw only more prune textured butts revealed under poor fitting swimsuits. Also the pool was not an Olympic sized as depicted on the billboards, but if you can imagine an extra big garden tub, then you get the idea. Thank God there were no bikini suits.

There were a few old geezers in the "pool," but I would have sworn they were using their Depends as arm floats.

Then the dining room appeared along the journey. A menu was posted for each day. Monday – Baked Chicken – Tuesday – Chicken Soup – Wednesday – Fried Chicken – Thursday Chicken Salad – Friday Chicken Livers – Saturday Chicken Terriyaki – Sunday – Roasted Chicken. That's enough chicken to raise the odds of getting the bird flu.

The environment of grounded trailers, which by the way, you could not own the land, but you rented the property 'til death do us part, did not impress me. After enduring four hurricanes in Florida the last year, I could only envision airborne trailers flying through the air with the greatest of ease, never to land as long as there was a breeze.

As we made our way from Geezerville, the land of extreme home makeover, I decided I was not quite ready to "geez most nunkily."

Sex Wise

TEACHING a speech class includes analyzing the audience. Questions like: What are the needs of the audience? What are the interests of the audience? What are the age, income, education, politics, religion, and the audience attitudes? These demographics help to make preparing a speech more comfortable and helps assure some success in positive feedback from the audience.

There is an exercise I use with my students to determine audience appeals. This exercise provides a profile of a certain audience, and the students are asked to work together in groups to work out an appropriate speech appeal according to the profile.

My favorite, because of the mixed feedback from the students upon completing the exercise, has to do with the following profile: A nursing home has invited some college students to speak on the subject of premarital sex. A dozen or so from the home have asked for this topic. Others in the home may attend. Ninety percent of the nursing home's residents are ages 65 to 105. Now the students are asked what type of speech they should prepare for this audience.

And, of course, there is the adolescent response with giggles about the elderly wanting to know about premarital sex. Usually students want to give a speech on what the audience can tell their children or grandchildren about premarital sex. Now think. How many elderly people in a nursing home would really want to talk about premarital sex with their offspring?

Many, unfortunately, never have consistent visits from their offspring. I note to the students that people in nursing homes are very lonely and that sex in these homes is not unusual. This pronouncement is met mostly with a "gasp", "ugh", or "you've got to be kidding!" Then I respond with a reminder about researching the topics before preparing a well-developed speech.

I teach them that statistics show that there is a rising concern for increased sexual diseases in nursing homes. Thus, the speech might just be about safe sex.

One student responded, "Oh, so this could be an Oral Presentation!"

Of course, the speech could take another turn like including the moral values involved in a sexual relationship without marriage. The purpose of the speech is not without challenges and discussions during the class time.

In any event, you can see teaching the young that the elderly are aged, NOT DEAD, is a major and awesome challenge, but most of the time a lot of fun.

ELDER COOL

YOU MIGHT BE ELDER COOL IF YOU KNOW WHEN IT'S TIME TO …

BE SEX WISE AND LOVING WITH OR WITHOUT VIDEOS

It might be time to be sex wise and loving if …

∞ Your partner wants to make love, and you empty

your pockets and find a mixture of antacid pills, aspirin, Imodium, and an assortment of a dozen other pills, but no Viagra. (Did you forget your Scout Motto – Be Prepared?)

∞ You have had a bedtime headache going on three years now.

∞ The past year you have been dreaming of Sofia Loren, and she has been dreaming of Sean Connery but the two never meet.

∞ You have been dreaming every night about living in a nudist colony.

∞ You pet your dog more than you pet your spouse.

∞ You have never been to the emergency room after sex to get oxygen.

∞ You gave up sex for Lent and Christmas, Fourth of July, Presidents' Day, Labor Day, New Years, Hanukkah, Kawanzaa and …

∞ You would prefer to play golf, go fishing, or get a manicure.

∞ You taped Monday Night Football over your 50th wedding anniversary celebration.

∞ You have not made love in the backseat of your car in a decade.

∞ You bought your 50th anniversary present at Dollar General, and it was not a prank.

∞ Your weekly Bingo game takes preference over your wedding anniversary.

∞ You haven't read the Song of Solomon together in bed for a long time. No videos are necessary. The word imagery is enough! (Anyone for Bible study?)

∞ Your last anniversary gift was a music box that played, "The old grey mare she ain't what she used to be."

∞ You insist going on the Judge Judy Show to mediate your marital problems.

∞ You think sexual intercourse is the only way to be intimate.

∞ You think spooning is eating ice cream.

∞ You no longer use your love handles.

∞ You think you are an animal when it comes to sex – that is a Canadian Moose who mates once a year.

∞ You really do think love and marriage go together like a horse and carriage, but lately you've been the horse's ass.

∞ You think Viagra should be used only to keep you from rolling out of bed.

∞ You think at your age you don't need to practice safe sex.

∞ You think remembering your wife's name is a turn-on.

∞ You think an elderly intellectual does not need sex.

∞ You would rather perform your own sexual gratification.

∞ You think sexual videos are underrated.

∞ You hang strobe lights in the bedroom to make like you are moving during sex.

Let Go Of Your Speedo

AFTER a thirty year ban New Jersey Beach now allows people to wear skimpy bathing suits. According to John Curran, Associated Press writer, April, 2005, "Not that everyone is cheering. It's often the older guys – the ones with beer guts, or wrinkly skin, or unsightly tufts of hair – who wear the tiny swimsuits." Maggie Creighton, 19, who works at a down town lingerie store and interviewed by Curran said, "The people you want to see in the Speedos, you don't."

Did you notice the words "older guys"? The elderly have a reputation at times for not dressing their age. Elder Cool dresses for one's age. A small amount of money can help one to dress casually, but not be a casualty.

Dressing up can be casual and can increase self-esteem and combat the stereotypes about us "older guys." Dressing smart represents a positive attitude about oneself. Self-esteem is at stake as one matures to a ripe old age, and smart dressing accentuates the positive feelings.

I remember shopping during the week before Father's Day in the Avenues Shopping Mall in Jacksonville, Florida, when two beautiful young girls spotted me. They came running with smiling faces. Immediately I raised my chest, smiled in response, and put on my special charm mask. "Sir," one of them asked, "Where did you get the shirt you're wearing?" I told them, and the other girl said, "Thank you so much. That is a beautiful shirt you are wearing, and we want to get our father one for Father's Day." And I said, "You're welcome," as my chest sank to the proper place, my smile turned upside down, and my charm mask fell off. In reflection, though, when you think about it, I was Elder Cool because I was wearing a shirt that was appropriate for my age. Be cool! Let go of your Speedo!

Just A Thought

"By the way, don't you think thongs are a bit too cheeky, no matter the age?"

JHG

Elder Cool

YOU MIGHT BE ELDER COOL IF YOU WHEN KNOW IT'S TIME TO …

Dress Smart

It might be time to dress smart if …

∞ You insist on wearing shorts, and you have chicken legs.

∞ You are wearing a dress that reminds one of a hospital gown.

∞ Your friends don't think you are dressed unless your zipper is down.

∞ You can no longer wrangle into your Wrangler jeans.

∞ You have so many rings around your shirt collar the traveling carnival wants to display your shirts as Alien Space Wear From Mars.

∞ You insist you look good with pants tight enough to see the imprint of your Depends.

∞ You date yourself by pretending to be Elvis with sideburns and wearing your shirt collar up.

∞ Your expanding pants no longer expand.

∞ You realized the difficulty of getting a tattoo on a prune-textured butt.

∞ You punched out the hair stylist because you thought it was her fault your hair turned blue.

∞ You and your spouse always wear matching clothes.

∞ You are not dressing to match the natural body modification that takes place while aging.

∞ Your clip-on-tie keeps falling in your soup.

∞ You insist on wearing a Speedo at age 80.

∞ You insist on wearing a bikini although the look-ers are laughing.

∞ Your cleavage is below your navel, but you insist on not wearing an uplifting bra.

∞ You have worn the same clothes so often that even the CSI could not find evidence if you were killed.

∞ You use rope for a belt.

∞ Your mix and match clothes do not match.

∞ Your pants legs are so short you could easily tread in two feet of water and not get them wet.

Eat, Drink, And Be Merry

HAVE you ever heard of Capparis spinosa? You have not unless you are a specialist in flowers and plants. Personally, I don't know one flower or plant from another. They all look like shrubs or petunias to me. Horticulture is not my thing.

A little research taught me more. After reading Ecclesiastes 12:5, I was intrigued by the words "… and desire shall fail…" Is this subject connected to failing sexual desire? No! The context of this verse finds the sophisticated author acknowledging the fact of growing old and the passing on of senses that once delighted him. Along with the losses of hearing and seeing, as aging controls us, is also the loss of taste. I discovered that according to *All the Plants of the Bible* by Winifred Walker, a stimulant arousing the taste buds comes from the plant known as Desire or Capparis spinosa. The plant is found today in Egypt and the Sinai Peninsula. The "young pickled buds" of the plant restore the "desire" to regain the taste of food.

Taste loss is not the only problem. Advancing age often requires a shift in food intake, and in today's world a major concern for "what" you eat is as important as "how much" you eat. My doctor warned me of trans fats and how detrimental the ingredients in food products are for the body. The risks of trans fats and hydrogenated oils (canola and soybean oils) require all ages to be more attentive to what we eat. Look closely at the ingredients (Nutrients are important, but ingredients are deadly!) in shelf products, and you will find enough chemicals to make a bomb! And, referring to bombs, the "killers" in our foods set off a heart explosion potential. When a "dangerous" ingredient like partially hydrogenated oils shows up in packaged foods, I get easily confused. Should I eat this or follow Willie Nelson's advice and put it in my car engine?

"Trans fats are a time bomb ticking in every one of us."

-Oscar London, M.D.

"Avoiding trans fats could add years to your life by preventing premature heart attacks."

-Walter C. Willett, M.D., P.H.D.

New label laws go into effect in 2006. Read the labels carefully as some will record no trans fats, but the product will have partially hydrogenated oils.

After my "stent" in the hospital, I was given a special diet. This did not work for me as I lost 3 to 5 pounds a week with tasteless foods. It reminded me of the time when my wife went on a diet; I lost 5 pounds! So I made a decision on reading the labels more carefully and controlling "what" I ate as well as "how much." Research suggested I eat the regular foods like butter, meats, and eggs, but eat less. I regulate my portions and keep the amounts in moderation. That is, I eat only one helping instead of the two or three, as I had in the past. My taste buds have improved, my weight is back to normal for my size, and I am merrier in my attitude.

I don't recommend this for everyone, but my Pop was asked at the assisted living home what he would like to suggest for improving the taste of the food. He said, "Add some fatback to the vegetables." The dietitian responded, "Mr. Green, that's not healthy." Pop quipped, "I'm 90 years old, I'd rather be happy."

There is something to being happy in advancing age. Ecclesiastes must have thought so as well because there are five versions in the book exhibiting variations of his famous verse, "eat drink, and be merry." Ecclesiastes 2:24; 3:13; 5:18; 8:16 and 9:7.

(I strongly advise reading the book, *Trans Fats*, by Judith Shaw, M.A., found in most drug stores.)

Olfactory Shortcomings

THE college classroom centered a discussion on olfactory, the act of smelling. This was a class on the effects of nonverbal communication on verbal communication. My students were discussing odors they like and dislike. One young man blurted out, "Old people smell." I looked at him with glaring eyes, and he continued, "Well, they do Dr. Green." And then, as if he realized my presence in the room, added, "I don't mean you Dr. Green!" One good thing about teaching college students is that once they trust you, regardless of your age, they are honest and open with their feelings. The young man's classmates were amused at his, shall we say, embarrassing moment!

I proceeded to ask him why he might have said what he said. He referred to past visits he had in a nursing home and about some older people he knew or had known. I responded with asking him to think about how difficult it is with aching joints, poor circulation, maybe arthritis problems, and other physical maladies that may prevent the proper and effective hygiene care so badly needed.

Odor problems are not uncommon for some young and old persons alike. Older people may find it is time to ask for help and face the humility that they need help to keep better hygiene treatment. Facing the humility of not being able to care for oneself is not easy. People need to be more sensitive to the elder needs. Elder Cool is facing and embracing the unmentionables.

Now, don't be too difficult on the young student. He is a great guy who is now married and, I'm totally certain has, at least due to the classroom experience, some understanding of elderly people in relation to olfactory shortcomings. Now where's my Old Spice? I know it is somewhere around here.

Pope John Paul II and Bill Clinton

AFTER Pope John Paul II died, several world leaders and former world leaders made comments relevant to the life of this great spiritual leader. Former President William Jefferson Clinton noted the many physical maladies the Pope had been challenged with during his lifetime.

The Pope had suffered a gun shot and had been diagnosed with Parkinson's Disease. Along with many other aging challenges, the Pope also had arthritis and breathing concerns. President Clinton noted in a news conference speaking about Pope John Paul II, "He was to be admired because he bore his physical maladies with grace."

Face the maladies and embrace them. Facing physical maladies without being in denial is not easy. Denial is the enemy of getting help when you need it. I could not believe I had heart disease, so I was a week late in returning to the hospital when I should have insisted on a catheterization the first time because I definitely knew something was not right. The first tests that cleared me led to my denial, but later I overcame the denial. I was lucky.

I can speak with experience about facing physical maladies with denial and the difficulty of overcoming this fault. Then to embrace a problem is also another struggle. Face and embrace. This is easier said than done.

When I was diagnosed with Inclusion Body Myositis, I was terribly frightened, and neither the want nor the need to embrace the challenge was within me. Later, much later, after talking with friends and others about the challenge, I was able to embrace. What a relief it was when I finally accepted. Facing and embracing one's physical maladies can help one moved toward becoming Elder Cool.

To me Pope John Paul II was a teacher, not just a preacher or Pope, but a real teacher in handling one's physical challenges. To me Pope John Paul II was Classic Elder Cool.

ELDER COOL

YOU MIGHT BE ELDER COOL IF YOU KNOW WHEN IT'S TIME TO …

FACE AND EMBRACE YOUR PHYSICAL MALADIES

It might be time to face and embrace your physical maladies if …

∞ You remove your dentures from your mouth to crack snow crab legs.

∞ You mow your lawn and do not realize the sprinkler system has been on the entire time.

∞ You missed the urinal the last three times you were in the restroom.

∞ You claim you were abducted and probed by Aliens from Mars and that's why it's hard for you to walk.

∞ Your voice mail says, "We'll call you when we remember where we are."

∞ You keep telling the same stories and jokes over and over again.

∞ You have taken more blood from the bloodmobile than you have given.

∞ Your head bedpost is propped up on a half dozen concrete blocks to deal with acid reflux.

∞ Your home nurse calls for backup.

∞ You travel to work, forgetting that you have been retired for five years.

∞ You carry a bottle of Ensure to all the BYOB social gatherings.

∞ You watch Denise Austin exercise for thirty minutes while sitting on the couch and now you're exhausted.

∞ You have stopped on the side of the road to relieve yourself five times in the last five miles.

∞ Like the commercial, you carry a portable potty on the back of your car.

∞ You remove your false teeth at the dinner table to explain how you floss.

∞ You talk about your constipation at the breakfast table.

∞ You've been drunk for three days and you claim it's for medicinal purposes.

∞ Your recliner has more gadgets than your car.

∞ You confuse 60 Minutes on CBS with Happy Hour.

∞ All your jokes refer to flatulence.

∞ You went snow skiing with your grandchild, and the Red Cross finally found you after three days.

∞ You played golf, and your three-iron went further than your ball.

∞ Your bathroom, bedroom, and your kitchen violates the county's health code.

∞ You can't hear your home security alarm go off if you are asleep or awake.

∞ You were playing Bingo, but kept on calling "Checkmate."

∞ You've been thrown out of Curves for spending more time on the floor than the machines.

∞ You talk a lot at the dinner table about your Metamucil cookies.

∞ Your hand to mouth cigarette smoking is your main exercise.

∞ Your attic and garage are full of toilet paper.

∞ You continue to leave the top down on your convertible when it rains.

∞ You made love, and after five minutes your wife said, "That's my navel!"

∞ You have a hand clapper key chain, but you can't hear your clapping or the response of the clapper.

∞ You did not catch the ending of the movie *Sixth Sense*.

Let's Talk Dirty!

"I'VE been talking about unmentionables for 30 years," says Cybill Shepherd, star of TV and the Silver Screen. Ms. Shepherd graced the cover of AARP magazine and has openly stated to the press, according to Knight Ridder Newspaper and as reported in The St. Augustine Record on April 7, 2005, "I tell women to talk to everyone – your family and friends and mothers and sisters, and especially your doctor, even if it is embarrassing."

Ms. Shepherd is referring to IBS (irritable bowel syndrome). She travels the country giving speeches as a spokeswoman for the "Amazing Women" campaign. Ms. Shepherd believes that talking will help people to get help. She has become a teacher with the goal to empower women to seek proper diagnosis and treatment for recurring constipation and sometimes diarrhea along with abdominal pain and bloating. Talking about the unmentionables by a celebrity will help others to seek the proper and needed help with less embarrassment. It's okay to talk dirty!

ELDER COOL

YOU MIGHT BE ELDER COOL IF YOU KNOW WHEN IT'S TIME TO …

TALK ABOUT THE UNMENTIONABLES
FINANCES
FUNERALS
FLATULENCE

It might be time to talk about the unmentionables if…

You can be embarrassed without blushing.

Hodgepodge of Scams

FINANCIAL disaster has come to be a serious concern for all ages, and the elderly are often trapped because of their age. Younger people can usually rebound, but the elderly are out of time in regards to starting over. According to the AARP, 12 percent of the population is 65 and over, however, they make up 40 percent of the financial fraud victims. Many of these targets are well-educated, but remain as vulnerable as other victims because so much fraud is committed over the telephone.

Financial concerns are often embarrassing to talk about, whether it is related to a scam, poor management of money, or simply a lack of money due to the rise in cost of living, but no increase of income. Unfortunately bankruptcy has been curtailed by law and hits the elderly poor the hardest. In the meantime, big corporations can file bankruptcy with the greatest of ease, and in the process, sometimes eliminate pension plans with the stroke of a writing pen.

Many seeking retirement in the near future have lost up to half or all of their means to retire without depending solely on Social Security. Add that to the hodgepodge of scams!

Who do you call? Call the FRAUD BUSTERS!

The SEC investor hotline is headed up by the Office of Investor Education and Assistance. There is a website: www.sec.gov/investor.shtml. This will help make your securities more SECURE. The hotline number is 1-800-732-0330. You can check the website www.sec.gov to make certain you have a broker that will not leave you BROKE. There is a great deal of confusion about the credentials of financial advisors. Their advice could lead to ADVERSITY, so check credentials carefully.

The lowest of the LOW are the elderly victims from the aftermath of hurricanes. Lower than a snake's belly are those who prey on already devastated elderly people. Above or right below these scam bums are the children of elderly sick parents, who steal from their own family.

I was asked to visit the home of a sick church member who had been diagnosed with terminal cancer. When I entered the front door it was not difficult to notice she did not have air condition in the middle of July. She kindly offered me some water to drink and apologized that was all she had to offer. I accepted the water.

Limping to the refrigerator and back, she took a chair and propped up her right leg. Then she began to tell me her story. Cancer had begun to ravage her leg and she was afraid of the consequences. During the conversation I discovered her financial plight. There was little food and drink in the house. She was in pain and she was financially broke. And, to boot, her two children had stolen some of her silverware, furniture, and appliances. Needless to say I had to take appropriate action. This tragic situation can be multiplied over and over again in the homes of poor, and sometimes, helpless elderly people.

Adding to the hodgepodge of scams is the inability to manage our own money. Rather than ask for help we scam ourselves by digging our own holes of debt. Digging out of unmanageable debt is like digging out of a hole in hell. The more you try, the higher your blood pressure rises. Scamming yourself is also a problem for all ages, but the elderly often have nowhere to turn and embarrassment sets in to the point of choosing suicide or bankruptcy.

Getting help should be provided without the stigma of feeling like a failure. Denial is the big enemy and sends some people to an early death due to financial stress. Seek help. After all, it is only money and there are a few services that can provide assistance. Don't be embarrassed, the Federal government cannot balance its budget either, and they pay "experts" millions of dollars a year to "keep" this American country, the good old USA, in debt. Your grandchildren, in the latest round of statistics, already owe $156,000 per child, due to the national debt. See, you are in good company! All of us can be taught a lesson to remember, and discover a peace of mind while moving toward Elder Cool.

IT MIGHT BE TIME TO TALK ABOUT FINANCES IF...

∞ Your credit card companies have your phone number on speed dial.

∞ You can't get your checkbook to balance due to writing your written check numbers in the phone book.

∞ You lost your checkbook, again.

∞ You use the Bible pages, and underneath the mattress, as your bank.

∞ You frisk your children and grandchildren for money when they leave the house.

∞ You have bounced more checks than Enron.

∞ Your money is fleeing so fast that you do not have enough time to pay attention.

∞ Your money doesn't go as far as it went yesterday because less is not more.

∞ Your Television Evangelist wants more money.

∞ Your money earns less at the bank as the bank's

earnings are increasing. In Monopoly it's called "Funny Money."

∞ Your money is disappearing at a rate faster than the income you receive. Your investments are privatized.

∞ Your money doesn't guarantee happiness, but you are happy when you have some.

∞ You can't afford to sin.

∞ Your money does not rule your life because your spouse rules your money.

∞ You think your money does make the world go around.

∞ Your money makes the world flat – flat broke.

∞ Your money can be summed up in one word – less.

∞ Your money does not equal the number of days in a month.

∞ Your money tree has been uprooted by a hurried cane.

A Funny Thing Happened After The Eulogy

I was watching C-Span TV one day and caught by accident, the humorist and former speechwriter for the late President Lyndon Johnson, Liz Carpenter. She stated her age as 82. I enjoyed her so much that I later purchased her book about speechwriting titled, *Start With A Laugh*. In her section of the book on Eulogies she says, "Humor can be an effective salve to soothe the wounds of grieving friends and family."

I have also delivered many eulogies in my lifetime, and humor has been a part of my content. However, sometimes the humor was not planned. For example, I had the service for an elderly gentleman many years ago at the cemetery of an old country church. This has been so long ago that what I remember most is he had a great sense of humor. The family had requested a graveside service since he had outlived many of his friends. At the conclusion of the service, as if it had been planned to make us laugh at a sad moment, a stray male dog came along and lifted his leg on the tombstone next to the deceased. This may sound irreverent, but I believe the old man must have been laughing in his heavenly destination with the thought, "Doggone, that was close!"

IT MIGHT BE TIME TO PLAN YOUR FUNERAL IF …

∞ You get a panic attack when you hear, "What do you want on your Tombstone?" and realize later the family is ordering pizza.

∞ You want the U. S. Congress to decide your fate instead of providing the family with a Living Will.

∞ You go to every funeral in town whether you know the person or not.

∞ You have planned a Happy Hour following your funeral service, but no other arrangements have been made.

∞ You have funeral plans for your pet, but you do not have plans for yourself.

The Butt of Old Fart Jokes

FLATULENCE has never been a favorite subject of mine. Bathroom jokes in movies and on the tube do not make me laugh most of the time. The term "old fart" really bothers me.

I have been called an "old fart" only once to my face that I can recall. One afternoon when leaving Home Depot, I walked across the parking lot to my car. I crossed through a handicapped parking space to save time since it appeared that rain was imminent and my legs were weak and bothering me. Just then an older challenged man was driving into the space. Upon seeing me, he blew his horn long and loud as if to get more than my attention.

So, out of a moment of fear I threw up my hands and said, "Don't hit me." He responded not only with the horn, but added, "Get out the way, you old fart." I guess it was evident by my body language that I was greatly shaken.

However, I didn't think I was an "old fart." My impulse was to tell him to get out of the car and put up his dukes, the "old fart!"

Calmness prevailed, and I moved to my car. Since I was physically challenged also, it would have been ridiculous to have seen two old farts fighting in the Home Depot parking lot. The fight would have resembled two one-legged men in a butt kicking contest!

This incident reminded me that I am a senior citizen, but if I want respect, I must show respect as well. Name calling, like "old fart," is degrading.

In reality flatulence is a challenge to many older people due to medication, irritable bowel syndrome, and other uncontrollable physical ailments. Of course, there are the controllable times too, so letting go at inappropriate times just might become a habit.

Yes, I do make fun of flatulence, but it can be a serious problem and embarrassing to talk about with others. But more people may understand better than you think about the unmentionables.

In the meantime, if you do not know the difference

between controlled and uncontrolled flatulence, in either case don't call a person an "old fart" and don't make the elderly the butt of old fart jokes! Be a better teacher than that.

IT MAY BE TIME TO TALK ABOUT YOUR FLATULENCE IF …

∞ Your flatulence was mistaken by the neighbors as a tornado.

∞ You are deaf and have flatulence.

∞ You notice people begin to move away from you and crinkle their noses.

∞ Your grandchild said, "Papaw, you farted."

∞ Your flatulence keeps blowing the covers off your bed.

∞ You open the windows and realize the smell in the house is not the town's paper mill.

Faith Factor Vs. Fear Factor

SOME studies indicate faith plays a major role in living a longer and healthier life. Others disagree on the premise that faith is just a crutch or a cane to lean on. Well a cane or crutch works for me when I walk! However, I believe faith is more than a "leaner on" when the times are tough. I never doubted my faith through the good or the bad times. In fact, I created most of the bad times myself. The exception might be my physical challenges. And who knows, my physical challenges may have had a connection to bad decisions that later became the emotional stress that later led to my physical disabilities. I believe that happens to many people.

Faith, for me, is a firm belief regardless of what is ahead of me in life and certainly for whatever happened to me in the past. That's my story, so to speak, and I'm sticking to it!

Waffle faith, that is waffling out of your responsibility just because you have been dealt an unfair hand in life, is weak at best. Life is unfair, and at times very cruel to those who seem to have the solid faith. In the book of Job, another piece of Wisdom Literature, Job demonstrates a solid faith. His family and friends accuse him of some type of sin and that he is being punished by God. Job is astounded that anyone would question his faith. The story goes that in spite of the horrendous condition in which he finds himself, he stills has respect for God. Respect is a more accurate word than fear. He doesn't necessarily like it, but his faith is intact. You know, with friends like the ones he had, he didn't need enemies.

"As God lives, who has taken away my right, and the Almighty, who has made my soul bitter; as long as my breath is in me, and the spirit of God is in my nostrils; my lips will not speak falsehood, and my tongue will not utter deceit. ... until I die I will not put away my integrity from me. My heart will not reproach me for any of my days. ... I will teach you concerning the hand of God; that which is with the Almighty I will not conceal."

(Job 27:2-11 - NRSV)

Job, through a solid faith, takes on life with what has been given and what has been taken away. He is realistic in that he is not happy about uncomfortable situations, but nevertheless, to hell with what others think, so to speak, God is in charge, and his righteousness and integrity will not falter. Job is a champion of faith even without the benefits of a good life. Job trusted in his faith not knowing the good life would be returned to him. Let's say Job encountered a faith check, and he passed. He had a right to be afraid when all seemed lost, but the faith factor overcame the fear factor. Job is a good teacher.

Whether one accepts the story of Job literally or as an allegory to be interpreted, Job speaks volumes about the faith factor and how fear, the strongest of emotions, can be controlled. I do not believe that the Creator gives us tests to prove our loyalty, but the tests of life do offer opportunities to strengthen one's beliefs and help us, perhaps change course in the direction life proceeds. I believe the ultimate will of the Creator is for life to be fulfilled whether the tests are fair or not. That is where the faith factor wins over the fear factor.

ELDER COOL

YOU MIGHT BE ELDER COOL IF YOU KNOW WHEN IT'S TIME TO ...

HAVE A FAITH CHECK

It might be time to have a faith check if ...

∞ Your Bible is fifty years old, but it looks brand new.

∞ You keep on lying about your age.

∞ Your favorite movie is *the Exorcist*.

∞ You smoked while watching Mel Gibson's *Passion of Christ*.

∞ You insist on playing Baby Jesus in the Church Christmas play.

∞ You still eat fish on Friday.

∞ You had to fish your bread out of the Holy Communion Cup.

∞ You make contact with your place of worship so seldom you are considered a visitor when you attend.

∞ You steal the pencils from the church pews.

∞ You fear you are going to hell.

∞ You stayed at the Holy Communion Table for a second serving.

∞ You don't need a medical plan because God will care for you.

∞ You think "going the extra mile" is something people should do for you, but not for others.

∞ Your hemorrhoids are the excuses for not going to church.

∞ You thought it was time to eat when the Pastor told the ushers it was time to pass the plate.

∞ Your hearing aid keeps you from going to worship.

∞ Your aluminum walker keeps you from going to worship.

∞ Your eyesight keeps you from going to worship.

∞ You try to pinch the lady usher at the worship service.

∞ You ask someone to move out of YOUR worship pew because you've been sitting there for fifty years.

∞ You don't go to worship because you get too cold.

∞ You don't go to worship because you get too hot.

∞ You give an elevated meaning to the word "grumpy".

∞ You go to church with your oxygen tank and ask, "Can I smoke in here?"

∞ You took the Baby Jesus doll from the manger in the Christmas play because it reminded you of your grandson.

∞ You ask the person sitting next to you if the Bible is a good book.

∞ You are not ready for the Creator to call.

∞ You have forgotten the words to *Amazing Grace*.

A Variation Of Psalm 23

MY physical challenges began to show up in my sports activities. I have always enjoyed playing basketball, softball, and occasionally golf. I was really saving my golf game for retirement time because I was mostly worse than other players. I remember losing a golf match to a 91-year old man when I was at the age of 51! After the game he disappeared, and upon inquiring where he went so quickly, I was told he was drinking a martini at the nineteenth hole.

After I turned 58, my golf game became a total disaster, and my only enjoyment of golf was being with my friends. Even my friends stopped watching me tee off I was so bad. My fingers could no longer properly grip the club handles. And the club would sometimes go further than the golf ball. Aches and pains in my neck, back and joints were becoming more unbearable after a golf match. Hollering fore, shooting six, and picking up on five was getting tiresome. So one day after shooting a one hundred-twenty on a par 72 course, I went home and wrote a variation of Psalm 23.

The Lord is NOT my Shepherd
when I am playing golf.
He does not allow me to lie in
green fairways, but I am
led into pools of still waters.

He does not lead me in
paths straight to the greens.
Instead I travel via the
roughs and sand traps.

Even though I ride in a golf cart,
I fear the next hole because
no one bothers to watch me tee off.
My number one wood does not comfort me.

A score tablet is prepared before me
in the presence my enemies.
My face is anointed with sun screen,
and my coke cup is empty from the heat.

I pray I will give up golf,
but then I think, "Surely there will always be
enough mulligans to follow me all the days
of my life, or I will dwell in the clubhouse forever."

Happy Hearts Club

MIDNIGHT and it was time to join the Happy Hearts Club. At the age of sixty-four, I was rushed to the hospital and straight to the ER. After numerous blood tests, which I passed easier than my doctoral exams, an EKG, a C-Scan, and other x-rays, all were pronounced negative. However, a week later I was back and would be included in the ten percent that passed the above tests. I was still having problems breathing and swallowing. The next step was a catheterization.

Ah Ha! Now I could join the club. This little exercise revealed one partially blocked artery, and a stent was put in place. I am grateful for my cardiologist and my family doctor and the hospital staff at Flagler, located in St. Augustine, Florida. I am also grateful for my wife, Kay, who drove the midnight run and was able to avoid getting a speeding ticket. The last time I saw her drive that fast was to a sale at the Outlet Mall in Saint Augustine, Florida.

Now joining the Happy Hearts Club was not a slam-dunk for me. You see the hospital nurses and doctors require a lot of blood. Each time I would fall asleep in the bed from hell, the nurse would wake me for more blood. "We need to draw some more blood", the lady with vampire teeth would say. I would, in turn, complain, and the nurse's response was always, I'm sure, in self-defense from my verbal blasts, "The doctor requires it."

One nurse actually referred to herself as Dracula. I did not doubt her. She missed a vein one time, and a balloon began to form on my hand. I was reminded of a story I had heard about a friend's mother losing her hand from such an incident. Could this happen to me? I could imagine telling the story, "Yes, I went to the hospital for heart surgery, and they amputated my hand." Actually I was having visions of having the mortgage on my house paid off by the hospital!

Another ordeal was getting the catheterization. I was placed on a very cold table in a very cold room. When my prune-textured butt hit the cold table, I came off the table so fast that I mooned the nurses. After the catheterization, the worst was yet to come.

The bleeding would not stop, and they placed a plastic vice-type instrument on my leg. The doctor then requested this device remain for six hours, so I could not move. I truly wanted to strangle the doctor by the end of the hospital stay. I do believe he had a sadistic strain in his blood system.

Loss of dignity ranks in the top three tests one must pass to enter the Happy Hearts Club, following the blood tests and catheterization. The backless dress one is required to wear, opens up to everything you never wanted others to know. When your wife laughs, you know others are rolling on the floor. In my case one strap was missing from the gown. I guess this was a case where Goodwill made a donation. Therefore, I was backless and strapless. This open door policy does help when you have to use the urinal and bed pan. I often thought that the ones who clean up must have the heart and soul of angels.

In spite of the trials and tribulations of hospital visits, the angels are there to serve, and my hat is off, and my pants too, to them and the dedication of their profession. I did not want to become a member of the

Happy Hearts Club, but the alternative for the time was unacceptable.

Elder Cool Rules
What's Hot

YOU might be Elder Cool if …

] You go back to school no matter what your age.

] You volunteer to serve non-profit organizations.

] You are the glue that keeps your family in touch.

] You assist someone in teaching Vacation Bible School at your place of worship.

] You read stories to children at the local library.

] You made someone mad, AND you apologized.

] You join the neighborhood watch team.

] You play with or spend time with your grandchildren.

] You visit people in the nursing home if you still drive.

] You deliver meals on wheels if you still drive.

] You teach illiterate adults to read.

] You write notes or send cards to homebound people for your personal pleasure or for your place of worship.

Elder Cool Rules
What's Not

YOU might be Elder Cool if you do NOT say to your children at inappropriate times ...

] I want to buy one more new car before I die.

] Well, I probably will not be around this time next year.

] I can't afford to give regularly to the church because I'm on a fixed income.

] I just bloat if I don't have a daily bowel movement.

] Growing old is not for sissies.

] I'm off to spend your inheritance.

] Your favorite movie is Grumpy Old Men.

] Hey son, do you remember the time when …

] I feel better so much better now that I had a bowel movement today. Now son, what were you saying?

] I have been constipated for days now.

] Let's watch reruns of the Lawrence Welk Show.

] I think your mother is losing her mind.

] Stop me if I've already told you this story.

] Somebody has to be the martyr around here.

] When I was young, I worked for $5.00 a day.

] Words you read aloud from the billboards and other signs as you go along for a car ride.

] Your mom and I still have a great sex life.

⟩ After all that education I paid for, it's about time you paid for dinner. (True! But don't say it!)

⟩ I remember when gasoline was 79 cents a gallon.

⟩ The trouble with this world today is that nobody has religion.

⟩ The world is going to hell in a hand basket.

⟩ What this country needs is another Great Depression like in the 1930's to make people appreciate what they have now.

⟩ The Neighborhood Watch Team is made up of a bunch of girly-men.

⟩ People who need people are the stupidest people in the world.

⟩ Scaring the little children in the neighborhood is great fun. (Some elderly people do this by removing their false teeth when children come by the house at Halloween.)

⟩ I think your father is losing his mind.

] You had better get right with Jesus. He's coming soon.

Granny D

I met Granny D when I was teaching at Jacksonville University. I had invited her to speak to my Speech class. Granny was ninety-four at the time. This was in the Spring Semester of 2004.

She gave an inspiring speech on why Americans should vote. The Fall Presidential elections were approaching. The class was very pleased with her enthusiasm and energy and knowledge.

Granny D's full-name is Doris Haddock. On February 29, 2000, ninety-year-old Doris "Granny D" Haddock completed a fourteen-month walk from Los Angeles to the Capitol steps in Washington, D.C., according to her book, *Granny D – Walking Across America in My 90th Year*. Granny D's purpose for the walk was to bring attention to the need for national campaign finance reform. She succeeded in getting the attention she was proposing.

In the cover section of Granny D's book, co-authored by Dennis Burke, she writes, "You need to have purpose in life, and you need friends. Friends often come from your commitments, your passions. If you are alone, it is usually a sign that you need to commit yourself to your beliefs or at least to a good activity. You need to give yourself away."

Listening and talking to Granny D, a retired shoe-factory worker and great-grandmother of twelve from Dublin, New Hampshire, I was totally engaged and thrilled with her intelligence and understanding of the world in which we live. She has embraced life with a purpose and lives with the hope that the United State of America can be a better place to live. Granny D teaches when she walks and talks.

Granny D is Elder Cool!

Elder Cool Views And News

○ Politicians across the country have investigated deceptive business practices targeting the elderly. You get invited to a free lunch by a group of investors only to find it is a set up to steal money from your savings. However, the most recent deceptive business practice relating to taking money from the elderly is State and Federal governments cutting Medicaid and Medicare.

○ You should start going back to the movies, they now have sound.

○ The most common cure used by the elderly to overcome the soaring costs of medical expenses is to, unfortunately, die.

Poetic Injustice: (JHG)

I passed a mirror hanging on the wall
Nothing important was on my mind,

At least not anything I care to recall.
I noticed in the mirror a Grumpy man.
His nonverbal appearance wasn't kind.

And this I just didn't understand.
So I rubbed my eyes to see.
And I'll be damned if it wasn't me!

○ NEWS ALERT: "If it sags, wags or drags I'm going to nip, tuck or have it sucked." Dolly Pardon

○ VIEWPOINT: According to *Harper's Bazaar* Goldie Hawn turned 60 in November, '05. She is quoted, "Who in the world would say you can't wear spaghetti straps after a certain age. That's insane."

○ Important Notice: Childproof bottle caps can be opened with a crowbar.

○ If you can no longer drive, putt.

○ If you can no longer walk, swim.

○ If you can no longer see, touch. (Be Careful).

○ If you can no longer talk, learn sign language.

○ If you can no longer hear, learn sign language.

○ After you learn sign language, teach it.

○ If you can no longer reach it, unlock it or turn it, invent it!

○ NEWS ALERT: Twiggy is 56! (Leslie Lawson) "I'm grateful for my lines of wisdom. … Worrying about getting older is a lost cause."

○ Anonymous Worry Words of Wisdom:

Why Worry?
There only two things to worry about:
Either you are well or you are sick.
If you are well, then there is nothing to worry about;
But if you are sick, there are two things to worry about:
Either you get well or you die.
If you die, there are only two things to worry about;
Either you will go to heaven or hell.
If you go to heaven there is nothing to worry about,

But if you go to hell, you'll be so damn busy shaking hands with friends you won't have time to worry!

○ MAJOR NEWS ALERT:

Six Saint Augustine, Florida Grandmas, ranging from ages 54 to 95, according to *The St. Augustine Record*, on February 14, 2006, Valentine's Day, walked into the local Air Force Recruiter's office to enlist and replace young soldiers fighting in Iraq. "This is a gesture of love," said Peggy McIntire, age 95.

○ MAJOR NEWS ALERT:

Now the government can determine your need for Viagra if you are a Senior citizen in the State of Florida. Officials caught the abuse of Medicaid purchases of Viagra for sex offenders. In order to correct the error, the Florida Legislature is removing Medicaid reimbursement for Viagra to everyone including the elderly. How about that? It's not enough to cut Medicaid for elderly, but the government can control your sexual urges by putting you in the same category as a sex offender!

○ NEWS ALERT: According to the AP on Tuesday,

November 29, 2005, Seventy-one year old Virginia McNeill will graduate on December 17, 2005, from the University of North Texas after three tries over a period of fifty-four years. Yes, there really is a Santa Claus, Virginia!

○ NEWS ALERT: Actress Adrienne Barbeau, best known for her role on *Maude*, had twins at the age of 51. Now the twins are six years old, and she is 57. She commented, "I was the only person in the hospital having twins and a member of the AARP."

○ VIEWPOINT: Actress Charlotte Rampling turned 60 this year. She says, "Hollywood has a 'barbaric' attitude toward older actresses." Recently she told reporters, "In Europe they understand wrinkles should not be a reason to be put away."

Bad Bobby Bowden

BOBBY Bowden is a mentor and teacher to many young people in college and others of all ages. He and his wife Ann recently celebrated fifty-six years of marriage with a bundle of children, six in their Seminole Quivers. If you don't know Bobby Bowden, you have missed a Golden Chief opportunity to be in the presence of a *bad* person. And if you are not hip-hop, you don't know that *bad* means *very, very, very good.*

I had the privilege and honor of meeting Bobby Bowden in Lake City, Florida, at the annual gathering of one of his many trips around the state of Florida representing the FSU football team as their coach. I had this honor for four years during the 1980's because I was asked to deliver the Invocation each year. His quips are faster than Chief Osceola at a spear-throwing contest.

What you see is what you get! He is genuine and humorous in the grand style of a true gentleman. Coach Bowden's football career record at this writing is 359 – 107 - 4. He has the most wins of any football coach in Division I college football. He has coached for forty years, and thirty of those years have been at Florida State University!

Coach Bowden has been a mentor, not only to his players, but to coaches as well. The coaches who learned from him have gone on to be very successful. In fact, they have been successful enough to defeat FSU too many times. Coach Chuck Amanto of North Carolina State served under Bowden and has defeated FSU three of the last five times and two of those times on the FSU football field. Coach Mark Richt of the University of Georgia was FSU's Offensive Coordinator and defeated Bowden in a post season bowl game. Tommy Bowden, one of his sons and Coach of Clemson University has spanked his father twice! Yet, Coach Bowden remains *bad*.

November 8, 2005, Coach Bobby Bowden turned 76 years old. Tommy sent his dad a birthday present. The younger Bowden said, "I sent him chocolate covered prunes and a box of Depends. I figured that'd cover everything." On Saturday, December 10, 2005, the Clemson Tigers defeated the Florida State Seminoles 35-14. That also covers a lot!

However, for Coach Bobby Bowden life is *More Than Just A Game*, the title of one of his books. In his book he states, "There has to be more to life – and a career – than one dad-gum championship." This is from a coach who has won two National Football Championships while at FSU. Coach Bowden also states, "… I'm more worried about how our players are going to be ten and twenty years from now, than I am winning the next game. I cannot, and I will not, sell my soul for football." These words followed an unusual losing streak of two games in 1989.

One day Coach Bobby Bowden will have to retire and he will be sorely missed, not just at FSU but to many people around the nation, and not just the Indian Nation. I expect to see him ride high into the sunset on the back of the Seminole mascot Renegade.

He is a man of Christian faith. I am very glad to have met *bad* Bobby Bowden, Elder Cool.

A Time To...

A Time To Lose ... (Your Mind)

Half-heimer's Disease – Forgetting only half of what you know.

Old man to old woman, "I know your age."
The old woman was very age sensitive and sharply quipped, "How do you know?"
The old man replied, "You told me yesterday."

"I have always endeared my wife by calling her Dumpling for the past fifty years", said the old man to a friend. "Why?" asked the friend. He replied, "Because I can't remember her name."

I feel like it is the morning after, but I can't remember the day before.

A Time To Hear ... (You Think?)

(As heard and told in a variety of ways.)

Three old geezers are sitting on the porch. One re-marks, "It's a windy day, isn't it?" Another responds, "No, it's a Thursday!" And the last geezer states, "Me too, let's get a Coors."

"I just bought a new hearing aid", the husband comes home to tell his wife. "Yeah", she says. "What time is it?"

A TIME TO TEAR (REND) ... (YOUR EMOTIONS)

Health Care: eye care, home care, dental care, care package, careless, care if I don't make the bathroom, caregiver, caretaker, and does anybody care? Health care emotions tear us apart.

Rip up your past mistakes and move on. It's time.

You have the answers, but sadly, no one ever asks you questions any more. You are also a warehouse full of knowledge, but you have lost the key to the door.

The old couple went to the doctor's office. The doc-tor said he was really concerned about their health and needed to have a urine and stool sample from both of them as soon as possible. They immediately took off their clothes and gave him their Depends.

A Time To Dance ... (A Real Senior Prom)

According to an article in the *Boston Globe*, April 23, 2005, Marion High School in Marion, Indiana sponsored a "real" senior prom for the senior citizens in the town. New dance steps were shared by the teenagers and the really elder cool. As we like to say at home, "You're never too old to cut the mustard!"

A Time To Love ... (And Keep It Up – Pun Intended)

An AP news report on May 28. 2005, reminds us sex is alive in the elder cool generations. According to the COA, Council on Aging, half of all Americans in the United States, aged sixty plus are sexually active. Seventy - four percent of the men and seventy percent of the women said they were satisfied with their sex lives. Shall we say, "Keep it up!?"

A Time To Die … (Everybody)

"We grow toward death. It is the last great adventure and we must prepare for it."

May Santon

When Bob Hope was asked where he wanted to be buried, he replied, "Surprise me!"

I hope Heaven is a lot like Barnes and Nobles.

(JHG)

"Hey, I love sleep, don't you?"

Kurt Vonnegut

A Time To Laugh …

Laughter does not have to be totally dependent on the changing conditions of the good times and the sad times. If a person is well-grounded in good friends, a loving family and a positive faith, then you have the springboard for good laughter.

"…I did not regard the use of laughter as a substitute for the medical care … in order to recover I brought a full range of positive emotions into play – love, hope, faith, will to live, festivity, purpose, determination."

Norman Cousins, Writer, Editor, as noted in *Psychology Today*, October, 1989, page 22.

The late Norman Cousins had severe inflammation of the spine and joints. He claimed that it was very painful to even turn over in bed. Cousins discovered his pain was seriously diminished with laughter. However, he was quick to communicate that laughter alone was not what led to his claim of being totally cured.

It is no secret that years of research provide insight to the positive response of a person's health in relation to a sense of humor. Scientific research indicates that after laughter, the activity of disease-fighting cells increase in accordance.

Humor is a means to better health for people of all ages. However, elder cool people might find humor even more beneficial due to all the aches and pains encountered as physical maturity brings on new areas of concern. Since laughter is a psychological response initiated by the brain, increase of oxygen in various organs of the body is stimulating. Heart rate increases and sometimes doubles, as if relating to some form of exercise.

Keeping Norman Cousins in mind, humor alone is not the key to withstanding aches and pains, but that a good laugh can enhance medical care and the sharing of needed faith, hope and love, thus, humor is stressed in these writings as the pivotal point in facing the good and bad times of health challenges.

PROFOUND THOUGHTS ON HUMOR

"A cheerful heart is good medicine, but a downcast spirit dries up the bones."

Proverbs 17:22. (NRSV)

"Laughter is the shortest distance between two people."

Victor George

"The kind of humor I like is the thing that makes me laugh for five seconds and think for ten minutes."

William Davis

"Life does not cease to be funny when someone

dies, as it does not cease to be serious when people laugh."

George Bernard Shaw

"Like Mark Twain I use humor against the racist."

Richard Pryor

A Time to Weep ...

Four women were arrested outside a grocery store in a village just south of Owasco Lake in the state of New York. According to the Boston Globe, September 19, 2005, the women were arrested for going topless on a downtown street. Two of the women were ages 54 and 61. Now my imagination tells me that was a time to weep!

A Time to Speak ...

To the Waitress at the Restaurant:

Do not call me baby. (God's sake, I'm 65.)
Do not call me honey. (My wife will hurt you.)
Do not call me darling. (My wife will hurt you more.)
Do not call me sweetie. (My wife will contradict you.)

Do not call me young man. (I am Elder Cool and proud.)

To the Waiter at the Restaurant:

Do not call me big guy. (NOTHING is big!)
Do not call me boss. (If so, you're fired!)

A Time to Heal ...

Have you offered someone you do not know a bottle of water, your coat, cell phone, umbrella, or visited someone you do not know in the hospital or prison?

A Time to Mourn ...

The revenge killing of another person.

The last episode of *Everybody loves Raymond.*

A Time to Hate ...

If you must, hate the action and not the person.

Bad TV commercials.

A Time for War ...

Stand firm against pre-emptive war.

"Wisdom is better than war, but one bungler destroys much good."

Ecclesiastes 9:18 (NRSV)

A Time to Kill ...

Is a violation of the Sixth Commandment.

"Am I my brother's keeper?" asked Cain.

A Time to Seek ...

And offer forgiveness.

(Don't go to your grave with guilt.)

A Time to Keep ...

Your mouth shut Pat Robertson.

Sometimes this is called a time of silence.

If you can't say anything good, don't say anything.

A Time to Sew ...

"A stitch in time saves nine."

(Unknown)

A Time to Plant ...

Estate Wills, Living Wills, Funerals, Vacations, Trips to loved ones, Date with spouse, Anniversary Celebration and you will pluck the benefits for yourself and others.

Ardis The Artist

I first met Ardis Hughes at a lunch counter inside a popular department store located in Saint Augustine, Florida. At first I observed him for about thirty-minutes as I was intrigued at the movement of his right hand. He was sketching the profiles of different people as they would sit and enjoy lunch. The people he sketched never knew or saw his magic pen. I went over to him and introduced myself and complimented him on his art work. I was astounded to learn he was 93 years old and would be 94 in January, '06. My wife was waiting on me to leave, so I told him that maybe we could talk at another time. Ardis said he came into the store most every day to have a bite of lunch and sketch people unawares.

Sure enough, about two weeks later, I went to the same store at the same time, and there was Ardis. I reminded him we had met earlier, and I asked if I could include him in my book about aging. He was gracious and delighted. I discovered Ardis lived in

Saratoga Springs, New York, about six months of the year and came to Saint Augustine for about six months of the year.

He grew up in a family that did not have the appreciation or knowledge for the cultural things of life. In 1930 when times were really tough, he went to New York City and studied art. Ardis said he enjoyed drawing nudes, and the first time he showed his father a nude drawing, according to Ardis, "the old man nearly passed out!" Ardis felt being an artist was in his "gut" and that was what he was born to do.

Ardis was able to squeak out a living and never married because he knew he was destined to move around a lot and he did not want the family under financial stress. In 1942, Ardis joined the army. It was World War II, and fighting had just begun. He told the officer in charge at the time that if they wanted to win the war, they would not make him a soldier. They took his advice and were smart enough to let him be the artist he was born to be. So he drew sketches, painting the scenes of war, and traveling around the world in the process. He was in the army until 1946 and spent his last year in Paris. He was bitten by the travel bug and spent the rest of his life sketching and painting in different parts of the world including, of course, New York City.

I asked Ardis, "What do you contribute to your longevity?" He jokingly responded with a canned answer he had given a thousand times to those who were always curious, "I drink a quart of whiskey a day and smoke five packs of cigarettes a day." That said, of course, with a sheepish grin and a twinkle in his eyes. I wasn't falling for that answer. Then Ardis said he did not know why he had lived so long, but one thing he did know was that being an artist and doing what he wanted to do had made him happy.

Then I asked Ardis his feelings about the purpose of life. He said, "I do not know. I have never thought about it. In my gut I knew what I was meant to do in life and I have been fortunate."

I said, "Well I believe the purpose of life is to be a teacher whether you want to or not and you teach each day even though you may not be in a classroom." Ardis responded, "Really!"

Ardis agreed to sketch me and would not accept compensation. Sad, but true, there is a major resemblance.

A Riddle Of Life

PSALM 49 is a unique piece of Wisdom Literature. The psalmist has wisdom to share about the problems of wealth and the certainty of death. As a teacher in the classroom of students the psalmist requires full attention with potent introductory words, "Hear this, all you peoples; give ear… my mouth shall speak wisdom… I will incline my ear to a proverb; I will solve my riddle to the music of the harp." (Verses 1-4 – NRSV)

The psalmist is curious as to why people covet the possessions of the wealthy. In his contemplation of death, he knows the end for all people, rich or poor, is death. The teacher teaches, "Truly, no ransom avails for one's life, there is no price one can give to God for it." (Verse 7 – NRSV) In other words, money does not buy one out of dying.

The psalmist also does not believe money buys one's happiness on earth and certainly not after death. "For when they die they will carry nothing away; their wealth will not go down after them. Though in their lifetime they count themselves happy… they will go to the company of their ancestors, who will never again see the light. Mortals cannot abide in their pomp; they are like the animals that perish." (Verses 17-20 – NRSV)

And so the psalmist gives a simple answer to the riddle of life: A pompous jackass dies forever!

Time Is Fleecing Me

Another day and time is fleecing me,
Soon my life will simply go away.
I feel like time is cheating me,
So I might not have another day.

Time seems like a dream to me,
And life is just a failing test.
I feel like time isn't what it seems to me,
So I must really teach my best.

Another day and time will be gone,
Life's cycle along with death is clear.
I must deal with pain and mourn,
Time is fleecing me and time out is near.

JHG

The Greatest Wisdom Speech

SOMETIMES referred to as the Sermon on the Mount, I believe this scripture offers the greatest words of wisdom. These words represent wisdom at its ultimate best. I wish Mel Gibson, or the likes of the film making industry, would put as much passion in delivering a movie on this speech as in the movie about the Passion of Christ. The Sermon on the Mount violates the work of Zealots for all generations before and since Judas.

Many believe Judas was a Zealot. That is, he was one who wanted to pressure Jesus to take military control as King of Israel and use his powers to overthrow the Roman Government and rule forever. Judas, forerunner to fast food service, wanted results sooner than later, and therefore, he believed, that by betraying Jesus, he would speed up the will of God.

Today, while people ignore the greatest words on wisdom, contemporary Zealots seek to speed up the end of the world. So-called defenders of religious values, pseudo-pietistic scriptural literalists, and misdirected flag waving idealists contribute to a Judas-style betrayal of the words of wisdom found in the greatest speech ever delivered. Revenge and murder do not take courage. Turning the other cheek takes courage. Praying for your enemies takes courage. Going the second mile takes courage. Being a peacemaker takes courage. Where are my literalist scriptural friends now? Being meek does not mean I am weak, but means I am strong enough to refrain from beating the hell out of you just because you did something murderous to me. Where are those who hunger and thirst for a world of peace through means of following the acts of Jesus? Where are the religious values that give one the strength to face the lions in a den of killing regardless of whether one lives or dies while standing up to the lions?

The Creator doesn't need help in speeding up the end of the world. However, it looks as if we earth-people are hell-bent on aiding the process. In addition to constant wars of hatred with biological and nuclear weapon possibilities, there are the crapulous environmental wastes and the unholy total ignorance of earth's disaster course.

Faster than the ups and downs of a tech stock, the earth is heated for disaster. (In case you thought "heated" was a misprint, think about global warming!) Is there hope? Yes, there is always hope due to the creation of free will. The will of mind and conversion of the heart to the greatest words of wisdom are still available and attainable. Each of the wisdom thoughts begin with "Blessed" in Matthew 5:3-12, which means in our language "Happy". There is still a chance for people to be happy and listen as "Then he began to speak, and taught them saying:

'Blessed are the poor in spirit, for theirs is the kingdom of heaven. Blessed are those who mourn, for they will be comforted. Blessed are the meek, for they will inherit the earth. Blessed are those who hunger and thirst for righteousness, for they will be filled. Blessed are the merciful, for they will receive mercy. Blessed are the pure in heart, for they will see God. Blessed are the peacemakers, for they are the children of God. Blessed are those who are persecuted

for righteousness' sake, for theirs is the kingdom of heaven. Blessed are you when people revile you and persecute you and utter all kinds of evil against you falsely, on my account. Rejoice and be glad, for in the same way they persecuted the prophets who were before you.'" (NRSV)

A Tribute To Pop

LAST Father's Day my first thoughts of the day began with my dad. I called him Pop. "Hey Pop. How are you doing?" I would say this each time I phoned or saw him. It's hard to believe he has been dead for nearly four years. Memories filled my heart and flooded my mind as I woke on this Father's Day. Pop died at the age of 92. He was a hard worker all his life. Pop's family was a victim of the Great Depression in the late twenties and early thirties. A fear of no income never really left his thinking most of his life.

Pop was not a gentle man but mellowed a great deal as he aged. He was not a formal school graduate but definitely had a PhD from the University of Hard Knocks. Pop lived mostly with other relatives from the age of 13, and school was not in his plans. Of course, being kicked out of school for rolling the teacher's son down the hill in a wooden barrel did not help his chances of remaining a student! Pop's mother died at an early age. His father remarried, and the children were passed around due to the economy and some neglect.

Pop spent a lot of time around sawmills growing up and working at the mills until he was 40 years old. He and mom moved often in order to find better jobs with sawmills. We lived in quaint little towns in Georgia like Camilla, Adel, and Boston. While living in Boston, at the age of 40, Pop decided to make a very courageous decision. He wanted to become an independent carpenter. Pop built and repaired houses for the next forty years. He couldn't read a blueprint, but he had the gift and talent to build, plumb, and place the electric wires in the right spot.

Pop was very proud of what he could accomplish and rightly so. If a person wanted a house, the person would tell Pop what he wanted, and he would sketch the plans on whatever paper was available. I once saw Pop sketch out a house plan on a brown paper sack! Sometimes My Mom would transfer the drawing to notebook paper and make some suggestions. Pop built over fifty homes and repaired hundreds in Boston and later in Monticello, Florida, where we moved when I turned 16. Pop and Mom lived in Monticello for twenty-eight years until Mom's untimely death at the age of 69.

Pop's talent was not bad for a man with no formal education and who had lost a thumb and finger on his gifted hand while working in sawmills. Pop just learned to hammer and saw with the other hand and eventually became ambidextrous. He taught me to use both hands in work and in sports. Sometimes down but never out, he had the true grit John Wayne could only play in a movie role.

Mom was a bright person who chose to give birth, nurture life, and channel her energy into home and motherhood. She worked outside the home only after I had graduated from high school and started college. Mom worked at a small dress shop in Monticello, Florida. Pop was not much for the tender moments in marriage or of parenthood. And though I knew he loved me, I never heard him say it until he was 85 years of age.

When I was at Jefferson County High in Monticello, Pop and Mom would attend my basketball games. I would be running down the court, and if the referee or the opposing team player did something Pop did not like, he would run up and down the sidelines yelling at him. Once I glanced to the sideline to see Pop flinging his hands in the air protesting the foul called on me by the referee. Yes, he loved me.

Pop and Mom were married for 53 years. Their marriage had many rock gardens as most marriages encounter, but when Mom died, he was completely lost, and it took years to recover to some degree. I had never seen him cry so hard or so often. He loved Mom.

Pop was a survivor and went on to work as a carpenter after "official" retirement until age 82.

His last work was a screen porch for a lady. He phoned to say, "Son, I told her I could only work six to eight hours a day." And that's Pop, John Lawrence Green, and he was Elder Cool!

At the age of 88, Pop drove his pick-up truck to the assisted living home in Dowling Park, Florida, and checked himself in. He phoned to let me know he was now home for the last move. Four years later Pop died. I certainly miss him and appreciate daily the good work ethic and true grit he taught me. After his death I put together some photos and hung them in my office at St. Johns River Community College and said aloud, "Well, Pop, now you are in college!"

A Tribute To Mom

MOM died at the tender age of 69 with colon and liver cancer. It seemed so unfair for a person who had refrained from any kind of alcohol or tobacco indulgences. She lived for eighteen months after the diagnosis. We did have moments to regain some of the closeness we had lost as time had passed so quickly with living our individual lives. Those eighteen months taught me a lesson about how life is so fleeting. In fact, during this period of time, Mom taught me several lessons.

Mom was the glue that held our small family together. She kept in touch with all the aunts, uncles, cousins, and her sister Pearl. Special occasions and family gatherings were coordinated by Mom. When she died, this dependence became more noticeable by the family. Members of the family who were sick or in trouble could always count on Mom to help. She was like a mentor to some and a teacher to others.

And Mom was a teacher to the community in the small town of Monticello, Florida. Her actions included total devotion to The United Methodist Church, gifts for children of the community, taking food to the elderly, and visiting the sick. This is not just a son bragging about his mom because the turnout at her memorial service at The Monticello United Methodist Church was sufficient evidence. People of all faiths, races, denominations, and a large number of children overfilled the sanctuary of the church.

Now Mom told me often how much she loved me and gave me a lot of self-confidence. Being the only child, I was spoiled by Mom but not in the way one might think. I was not lavished with presents or anything I wanted. In fact, I didn't realize how poor we were until later in life. However, we never went without food, shelter, or clothing. I started work at an early age and purchased many of my school clothes, but poor was never in my thoughts or vocabulary.

Mom spoiled me with attention, overprotection, and at times love. What a way to be spoiled! She was a disciplinarian and taught me to obey adults and especially teachers and ministers. It was not unusual for Mom to take away privileges at the drop of a hat when I went against her wishes. I was good most of the time in the home and in the schoolroom, but when I was outside, according to my second grade teacher, I was a "holy terror"!

I was trained with discipline to the point my Mom could look at me with laser eyes so piercing that they could cut open a can of beans. I knew immediately that if I did not behave, she would take me to task later.

Mom taught me the meaning of God's grace, human love, and Christian forgiveness. And even when she knew I was a total jackass in some of my decision making, she loved and supported me with love. Later on in life when I was a young adult, she told some people I had never done anything wrong. The people laughed and rightly so! Mom knew I had done many things wrong in growing up, but she had forgiven and forgotten.

Much later on in my adult life and after my Mom's death, I made a horrible decision that was more than border line unethical. It has taken many years to reconcile the mistake and make the proper amends. Months before the catastrophic results of my decision, I dreamed of my Mom. She was in full view and as beautiful as I remembered before she became sick. She approached me in the dream and embraced me with a mother's love, a hug that was as real as life. In fact, it took me a while when I awoke to discern that it was not real. The entire day following the dream I felt a feeling of peace I have never felt before or since. It was the continued memory of that dream and that day which gave me some of the strength I needed to get through the roughest months of my life just ahead of me. Call it what you may of that dream experience, and even though Mom had been dead for over twenty years, it was an amazing spiritual happening for me.

Mom and Pop were married for 53 years, and some close friends thought Mom should have received the Congressional Medal of Honor! However, Mom also loved Pop in spite of his failings. They were married when she was barely 16, with permission of her parents, and Pop was 23. Times were rough during the Great Depression, but they managed to be survivors against what faced them and contributors in an effort to help others.

Mom taught us all to be courageous. After the diagnosis of cancer, she received chemotherapy, and the cancer was in remission for about six months but then came back with a vengeance in a short period of time. A few weeks before Mom died, she told me it looked like she wasn't going to win the fight. And then she added, "I'm glad I'm going to be cremated. This way I will get the last laugh on burning this thing (cancer) up."

The family will always be grateful to The Reverend Tom Derrough, at that time the Pastor of Monticello United Methodist Church. He helped Pop through some difficult times and was present on the night of Mom's final hours. He said at her Memorial service that "Ollie Green never taught in a classroom in Monticello, but she was a great teacher of life and death." And that is a snapshot of my mom who was Classic Elder Cool.

Credentials

I HAVE INCLUSION BODY MYOSITIS
(Irreversible loss of muscles in the arms and legs)

I HAVE IRRITABLE BOWEL SYNDROME

I HAVE RHEUMATOID ARTHRITIS

I HAVE TINNITIS

I HAVE DRY MOUTH & BURNING DRY EYES

I HAVE HEART DISEASE

I HAVE TROUBLE TYING SHOES

I HAVE TROUBLE TYING TIES

I HAVE TROUBLE BUTTONING BUTTONS

I HAVE TROUBLE OPENING CANS &
BOTTLES

I HAVE TROUBLE OPENING CHILD-PROOF
MEDICINE CONTAINERS

I HAVE TROUBLE WALKING WITHOUT FEAR
OF FALLING

I HAVE EXPERIENCED PANIC ATTACKS
WHILE DRIVING OR WHEN CROSSING A
STREET

I URINATE A LOT

I HAVE HIGH BLOOD PRESSURE

I HAVE HIGH CHOLESTEROL

I HAVE SEVERE ARM, LEG, NECK AND BACK
PAIN

I OCCASIONALLY EXPERIENCE BLURRED
VISION (Especially when I look in the mirror.)

I HAVE ACID REFLUX

I TAKE THE PURPLE PILL

I TAKE PLAVIX

I HAVE TROUBLE STAYING IN THE
MISIONARY POSITION

I HAVE A SENSE OF HUMOR

I LAUGH A LOT

I ENJOY COMEDY CENTRAL

I ENJOY PEOPLE OVER AND UNDER FIFTY

I AM A TEACHER

I REALLY ENJOY MY STUDENTS

I HAVE A LOT OF FRIENDS

I HAVE FAITH

I HAVE HOPE

I HAVE LOVE

I AM IN LOVE

I HAVE FREQUENT SINUS INFECTIONS

I AM LACTOSE INTOLERANT

I AM SIXTY-FIVE YEARS OLD

I AM HAPPY MOST OF THE TIME

I AM LUCKY

I AM BLESSED

I WAS BORN INTO GRACE

I FACED DISGRACE

I FOUND AMAZING GRACE

About the Author

DR. John H. Green is presently a fulltime teacher at St. Johns River Community College in St. Augustine, Florida. He teaches Speech Communications. Dr. Green received his Ph.D. from Florida State University in 1982. He was recommended to *Who's Who Among America's Teachers* in 2003-04 and 2004-05 by students from Jacksonville University, Jacksonville, Florida and the Community College. Dr. Green has spent the last forty years working in churches and schools. He also has a Master Degree of Divinity from Emory University in Atlanta, Georgia. Dr. Green is the author of numerous newspaper and magazine articles. He is married to Brenda Kay Miller Green. Kay works with the local St. Augustine Council on Aging as Coordinator of Volunteers and Program Development.

Dr. Green says, "College students keep me thinking young and inspire me to keep on learning. Some people believe these students are America's future, but I think in terms of them as America's present as well. Deal with these minds in the present, and you will make the world safer for the future. I struggle to engage myself with the students in a way that teaches them to think 'outside the bun', and in so doing, creative minds will bring us a destiny of a hope that will never die. I teach that humor is a great source for loving to learn, that humility will help keep a balance on the perspective of life, and that serving humanity is the ultimate goal."

www.ingramcontent.com/pod-product-compliance
Lightning Source LLC
Chambersburg PA
CBHW051421280526
45785CB00003B/1109